In the Garden

A.K. Harlan

Copyright 2025 by A.K. Harlan

Copyright 2025 by A.K. Harlan

All rights reserved.

Images by A.K. Harlan

Published by Oak Branch Publishing

ISBN

979-8-218-89255-5

By the same author

Collected Stories

Collected Stories II

Journey

Foolish Wager and Other Stories

She greets the day wondering what it will have in store for her.

Recently, her life has been complicated yet she knows that in the garden she will seek and she will find tranquility. Yet tranquility was not enough; she needed to engage her mind in the pursuit of knowledge.

She sought what symbols the various flowers were associated with and how this symbolism is associated with her.

The following are the many flowers she has photographed and she has grown to love more deeply by finding their meanings. She learns that many of the flowers exhibit the same symbolic meanings. As she studies her many photographs, she chooses to research them in the order in which she took them. She feels these symbols will reveal her hidden dreams and wishes and will give her a deeper vision of herself.

Sitting silently in her garden, she came to some conclusions about her life and how she would move forward, would travel, would see something of the world.

The first photo in her collection is of the pink dogwood blossoms which can represent love, passion, and affection, especially in the context of romance. As she gazes at the photo and the symbols it represents she thinks of past loves, and how she has grown emotionally due to some of her romantic encounters. She also finds that the blossoms can carry deeper meanings of rebirth, resurrection , purity and endurance. She realizes the symbol of strength is due to the tree's resilient nature

She feels such joy when the tulips bloom for they symbolize perfect love, rebirth and new beginnings but, she learns, their meaning varies significantly by color. Red tulips represent deep love, which she has known, while pink tulips signify affection and care, which she has also known. White tulips mean purity or forgiveness which she finds in common with many other white flowers. They can also be sent for condolences. Remembering having received a bouquet of all these colors brings a smile to her face

Looking at this picture from a Botanical Garden in Hawaii, she wants to visit another Botanical Garden maybe in Florida.

The lovely Narcissus was her next photo and the initial meaning of new beginnings, rebirth and the arrival of Spring pleased her. She did however, find the second meaning troubling as it was unrequited love, vanity and even death due to the Greek myth of Narcissus. Thinking it best to focus on the positive aspects she chose to ignore that the unrequited love and vanity struck close to home.

Her cheerful mood returned as the next photograph of a Sunflower represents happiness, optimism and the act of following light or seeking the positive. She delights that this includes loyalty and strong bonds and she begins thinking of those she holds dear.

Her belief and fear of evil spirits is assuaged knowing that Chives has meanings of protection against evil spirits and negative energy and also offers purification and healing properties. They are also associated with long life, prosperity and breaking of bad habits. Perfect, she thinks, these compliment the other flowers in the garden.

A reminder of Spring always accompanies the Azalea, brilliant in color with full blossoms and leaves, it symbolizes temperance, beauty, abundance and femininity. Agreeing with the beauty and touched by the femininity, she also finds she prefers the European folklore that says the plant has magical flowers connected to fairies and mystical beings.

Merely the name, Bleeding Heart, drew her in as she found the symbol ranges from everlasting love and deep emotional connection to sorrow and lost love.
She allowed herself to think that she had known both. Her reading disclosed that the contradictory meanings stem from the distinctive heart-shaped flowers with a drop-like structure at the bottom which can be seen as either a symbol of love or a symbol of a wound.

As she gazes at the pink Daylily photograph, she again finds the same symbols of beauty and prosperity but also the fleeting nature of life. She learns it also represents admiration and gratitude. As always, she thinks of her life and that eventually she will die just as the lilies in the Fall.

Now, she regards the Orange Daylily which symbolizes enthusiasm, passion and confidence. She is struck that it is linked to strong emotions like pride and in some specific cases, hatred. Sighing, she knows she has never truly known hatred.

She is happy to see that the Red Hot Poker plant represents strength and determination. The google search says that the unique flower is prized for it's vibrant fiery colors. She agrees as it is the striking focal point in her garden landscape. Her determination has always seemed to send her in the right direction in pursuit of a desire.

Searching for the orange Chrysanthemum she finds they symbolize happiness, excitement, and enthusiasm. They embody a sense of vibrancy and are often used to celebrate achievements and express positive feelings like joy and warmth. She promises herself they will adorn her front porch in the Fall.

She then sees the white Globe Amaranth photograph and finds that it symbolizes immortality, enduring love, and friendship all of which she found quite appealing. Along with this, she found the flower's amazing ability to last as long as 3 weeks in a vase or years when dried. In the Victorian era they were given as a way to say, "My love will never die."

Interested further, she next discovers the symbol of the purple Globe Amaranth and finds it can also represent friendship, strength and vitality. It differs only from the white flower in that its strength is endurance,

Cheered by the Purple Petunia's symbols, she notes it is fantasy, enchantment, grace, royalty, respect, admiration and mystery. She vows next Spring there will be many planters filled with these beautiful flowers.

Echincea has always been an important flower for her to have in the garden. The symbols include strength, healing and resilience due to its medicinal history. Of course, she tells herself they symbolize health because they attract pollinators like bees and butterflies to the garden. Another one to be sure and cultivate in Spring.

Her yellow Daffodils were always a delight as they naturalize and fill a corner of the garden. Like some of the other flowers, they represent joy, new beginnings, hope and the end of Winter and start of Spring. They are also associated with friendship, good luck and prosperity. The bright yellow flowers always lift her spirits.

She was finally able to grow some Daisies and, of course, photographed them. It had been difficult for her to get them started. Their sign of innocence, unity, and new beginnings reflects their "day's eye" name. She remembers the expression "pushing up daisies", but quickly dismisses the thought with the cheerfulness and hope found in the flower's simplicity.

The pink peony was a start from a friend's garden. She found it ironic that it meant romance, grace, admiration and gratitude. As it is often associated with good fortune in a happy relationship, she knew that was something she only longed for and doubted in reality.

As always the purple Iris represents royalty, admiration and wisdom. She knows that it's royal color has been linked historically to royalty due to ancient Egyptian art and it's association with the Greek goddess Iris whom connects it to valor and a "messenger of the Gods."

Red Athuriums symbolize love and passion. She remembers having taken this photograph while visiting a Botanical Garden in Hawaii. At the time, she did not know its symbolism.

She is familiar with the symbolism of the red Roses being love, romance and passion. She finds it is also a symbol of desire, courage, beauty, respect and devotion. She is reminded of the long stem red roses she received when she turned 16.

She again finds photographs of the orange Daylily and remembers its symbol of enthusiasm, passion and confidence. She takes pride in her confidence as she moves forward in her life.

As she looks at the Blazing Star, she finds that they have varying symbolism, in Freemasonry they represent divine guidance, and spiritual perfection and in some native cultures, symbolizing pride, resilience and beauty in Islam they are described as lamps or missiles to ward off demons.

She again finds that the white Daylily represents purity, innocence and rebirth. They represent the fleeting nature of life as each daylily flower blooms only a single day before being replaced by a new one as a symbol of transformation and renewal.

The purple Morning Glory is also a favorite as she plants them every year and has them growing on her garden gate. The flower represents nobility, royalty and beauty. She notes that it also means the fleeting beauty of life to which she acknowledges.

She does believe the red Zinnia represents love, passion and strong emotional bonds representing the steadfastness of family ties. All of these traits she has known through joy and sorrow.

When she sees the lovely photos of the Black Swallowtail on her pink zinnia, and then as a Fritillary on another pink zinnia she thinks of the pink zinnia's symbolism lasting affection, romance and deep admiration are justly named. She feels the pink color is a favorite of these colorful visitors.

The orange zinnia is a symbol of enthusiasm.

Finding the anemone her next photograph, she also finds its symbolism conflicting. It begins with anticipation and protection then next involves forsaken love and death. It derives from Greek for "wildflower". She notes the dual symbolism as the joy of spring and the sorrow of loss.

As she studies the purple and pink impatients she finds they are a symbol of maternal love, something which she has never known, but known also as the symbol of grace and gentle affection of which she has bestowed on others.

The photograph of the pale peach daylily with raindrops on its petals was a lovely reminder of that rainy day. She also remembers it is a symbol of the sweetness and fleeting beauty of life. She feels this is a nearly perfect photograph.

The close-up of the blue Morning Glory was one she took pride in having grown and photographed. She feels it appropriate that it represents trust, respect and affection particularly in the Victorian era. It is linked to deep emotions due to the blue color. This makes her happy to have them growing on her garden gate.

The Moonflower photograph was taken on her front porch as she had them growing up the trellis. She is pleased that they symbolize mystery, magic and romance because they bloom at night. They represent transformation or hope as they flourish at night.

The beautiful sunset Rose's symbol is enthusiasm, desire and fascination. Which bridges the gap between friendship and romance, and she thinks of him wistfully.

Much pleasure is derived from the yellow Ornamental Gourd blossom representing fertility, prosperity and the life cycle. They embody the potential for new life as they grow up the garden fence.

While the white Birdhouse Ornamental gourd blossom denotes purity and growth, she learns that they have a relationship with specific pollinators which also contribute to their special symbolism.

She silently regards the white zinnia blossom symbolizing pure goodness and new beginnings that she longs for in her future.

As she gazes at the red Rosebud representing young love, purity and beauty that is still developing, she remembers her first love, young love, and cherishes these feelings.

The salmon colored Hibiscus signifies hope and fresh starts, also with feelings of friendship, rejuvenation and enthusiasm. As always, she guards her hopes carefully.

The yellow Coreopsis brings cheerfulness, love at first sight and is associated with optimism. These are all emotions she wants to cultivate just as she does her garden. The idea of love at first sight enchants her.

The purple Aster from her garden symbolizes wisdom, stability and admiration. They represent royalty and respect. They are also associated with patience, faith and elegance. These attributes do not surprise her about the flower. The purple color adds layers of meaning like mystery and dignity.

Her white Daffodils represent purity, innocence and a moving away from vanity that signifies spiritual growth and renewal. Her vanity has never really been an issue, and she longs for spiritual growth in her life.

The Dahlias in her friend's garden symbolize elegance, inner strength, commitment and change. The specific meaning can vary by color. The pink her friend has represents kindness and the white for new beginnings. All this she finds true of one of her oldest friends.

She arrives at the beach resort in Florida with plans to visit a botanical garden to capture more photographs of the beauty she finds in flowers.

In the resort's pond were Waterlilies which symbolize rebirth, purity, enlightenment and beauty across different cultures. She finds that they represent resurrection because they close at night and open in the mooring and enlightenment for rising from the mud to bloom. She also found that other meanings include sun, creation and life itself especially in ancient cultures. Next stop, the botanical garden.

Greeted by the sign, she enters, camera in hand, to photograph some tropical flowers. She plans to spend joyful hours here.

How fitting she thought that the first plant to see was a Pink Mimosa tree that symbolizes femininity, sensitivity and new beginnings. She smiles when she discovers the tree is associated with happiness and healing.

The next tree picture she saw was the Red Powder Puff tree that represents vitality, celebration, and prosperity due to its bright fluffy flowers. She recalls the delight she felt viewing the well tended tree.

The Golden Shrimp Lantern she found interesting and then even more so as it does not have a traditional meaning.

With regard to the White Candle plant, she finds it represents two different plants. Both plants' symbolic meanings are related to the color white and the shape of the flowers.

The following photograph of the Blue Ginger plant she finds represents beauty and diversity. Also listed is their symbolism of resilience, healing and prosperity.

She is again struck with yet another plant symbolizing prosperity.

She asked herself why she took the photograph of The Lady of the Night as it had already begun to fade, just like so many of us she thinks sadly.

Upon finding that Bougainvillea symbolizes a variety of things depending on the culture, she researched further finding it symbolizes passion and welcoming visitors, however it also symbolizes beauty, resilience, peace and strength with its thorns often signifying protection. These need to be in the garden as well, she thinks.

Just the name of the Pagoda Flower evokes images of purity and the ephemeral nature of life. It represents devotion. In some cultures, it is called "crown of Lord Krishna".

She enjoys the symbolism of the Starfish Cactus as it represents endurance and resilience due to the ability to survive in harsh conditions. She asks that everyone be able to survive in harsh conditions.

The Madagascar Ocotillo is also known for its resilience and its adaptability as well. Again, she asks that all people be able to adapt to their everyday conditions.

Studying the Yellow Aphelandra's photograph, her research revealed a symbolism for vibrancy, distinction and prosperity. Due to its striking appearance, it represents adaptability and resilience while bright colors can be associated with general happiness and joy.

Researching the King's Mantle flower, she finds the name primarily stems from its appearance, evoking royalty, majesty and the "King's mantle" due to its striking purple color and shape, which she found charming.

The Golden Candle plant represents good fortune, prosperity, and wealth due to its golden color. As is similar to other yellow flowers, it represents resilience, vitality and positivity as it is a vibrant sun-like color. She is reaching the end of the photographs and wants to complete the research she has begun.

She found no common name for Neoregelia concentrica and liked its meaning of hospitality and warm welcomes. She loves to entertain and usually has an idea for a future get-together.

The pink orchid tree's symbolism includes beauty, grace and femininity. She found it interesting that it is also known as the Hong Kong orchid tree and symbolizes strength, purity and the unique identity of being Hong Kong City's official flower.

The next two flowers she had no name for and was disappointed that she only found a few in the Tropical Flowers book she purchased.

The parrot bid her goodbye as she exited the Botanical Garden. Naturally, he was photogenic.

She bids goodbye to Florida, the beach and the Botanical Garden grateful for the opportunity to have spent some time there yet, she is happy to return to her home and find peace in the garden, with plans for future planting.

Additional offerings from Oak Branch Publishing

Gregory Ferris	One Hundred and Sixty-Four Buttons
Gregory Ferris	Zoe: An Act in Two Plays
Gregory Ferris	Inutile
Gregory Ferris	Them Ain't the Breaks
Gregory Ferris	La Petite Masion du Chocolat
Gregory Ferris	COVID Confinement, or Much A Flu About Muffin
Gregory Ferris	Traquant Dieu
Gregory Ferris	Witches' Brew
Gregory Ferris	Shoot the Messenger
Gregory Ferris	Rendez Vous
Gregory Ferris	La Famille Bilingue and A Simply Missing
Michael Kessler	The Erastist
Julie Segal	The Silent Shofar
Antje Simunac	I Will Dance Again

www.ingramcontent.com/pod-product-compliance
Lightning Source LLC
Chambersburg PA
CBHW041607220426
43666CB00001B/9